Beauty Beneath The Surface

Shanita Rogers

Copyright © 2017 Shanita Rogers

All rights reserved.

ISBN: 978-0-692-88642-7

DEDICATION

I dedicate this book to my savior, Jesus Christ the one who loved me enough to offer His life so that I could live!

Thank you to my husband Antwan Rogers for your faithfulness throughout the years. Thank you for encouraging me to release my gift of writing.

Jala, Taylor & Christian, my children, you have served as a constant reminder of why I am here. I am honored to be your mother. Imani and Antwan Jr. thanks for allowing me to be a part of your lives as Ma'Nita.

To my wonderful parents, Jeremiah & Priscilla Street, thank you for being the greatest parents possible!

To my grandmother, Shirley McCall I am forever grateful for you loving me every single day of my life! You mean the world to me.

To my sister Keosha, brother Jeremiah Street Jr, sister in law Mary Street and to all of my nieces & nephews thank you for your support!

To my extended family (Street's, McCall's, Hill's, Rogers & anyone I missed), friends & church family who have supported me in any endeavor I am so appreciative!

ACKNOWLEDGEMENTS

To my sister friends Brandy Simmons, Capresha Caldwell, Susii Dobresnski & Pastor Sharon Walker I am forever thankful for you being present and believing in me.

To Pastor Al & Mrs. Tava Brice you are such a blessing to the kingdom of God! Thanks for having a heart for people and fulfilling the call of Christ.

I want to acknowledge women who have been a blessing to me over the years as they operated in their calling and demonstrated the Proverbs 31 woman: Mrs. Marilyn Gool, Pastor Nancy Dufresne, Sandra Waller, Pamela McCray, Joyce Meyer, Christine Caine, Pastor Cynthia Brazelton, Dr. Dee Dee Freeman, Heather Lindsey and Nettie Hood.

To Stephanie Rodnez thank you for walking in your gifting with passion. What a blessing you are to me and others who are writing!

TABLE OF CONTENTS

	Acknowledgments	v
	Introduction	viii
1	Pretty Ugly	1
2	College Girl	9
3	Study Guide	21
4	Exit Here	27
5	The Rescue	41
6	Not Again!	50
7	Blending	57
8	A Price to Pay	62
9	Instruction Manual	87
10	Problem Solver	101
	Action Step	108
	30 Daily Affirmations	112
	Prayer	141

BeYouty

INTRODUCTION

As a married woman I have fought loneliness. As a public speaker and workshop host I have felt like a failure. I was blessed to birth three beautiful children into this world and at times still believed I was unaccomplished. What amazes me is how often I opted to downplay all that God has blessed me to experience in my time on this earth. Surely I am the only woman in this world that has done such things? The truth is most women at some time question their existence and purpose. Even some of the most successful people often doubt themselves and the gifts that God has placed within them. Why is that? In this book we will take a walk down a path that is very familiar to us all. I will share my journey of doubt, faith, encouragement and discouragement. I allowed layers upon layers of confusion to blanket my heart.

The cover ups prevented me from seeing all of the wonderful attributes that God designed for His glory. Wearing masks forced me to live a life in which I attempted to please others. It was an act that I became accustomed to living. But for some reason I was never quite able to master the task of people pleasing. It wasn't until I saw the Beauty Beneath the Surface that I realized that life satisfaction would come as a result of pleasing God. Not only would I be blessed but others would as well.

BeYouty

CHAPTER 1-PRETTY UGLY

Sitting upright on my bed, all alone, in the dark, staring at what I knew to be the four white walls of my room. I thought about everything I didn't have. No one wanted me to be around. At least that's what my mind had convinced my heart to believe. With tears flowing down my face I walked out of my room, down the hall past my parents' bedroom and then the bedroom that my sister and brother shared. "I can end it right now! I'm finally going to accomplish my goal. I am going to settle this once and for all." I made it to the kitchen doorway, turned around and walked back towards the bathroom. I entered... With the light on and door closed I just stared at myself in the mirror still in tears. "I hate the way you look! Your lips, your cheeks, your nose, your teeth... You're not pretty. You don't really have friends. Your life is not worth living. Just go ahead and do it!" I felt like the pretty ugly girl. I was a well-behaved child who didn't feel pretty at all. That night, at age 12 I found myself struggling with being suicidal for the first time. My mind and emotions were telling me to stab myself. My plan was to go to the kitchen to find a knife. However, there was something greater than my mind that won that night. All of those Sunday morning church services, Sunday afternoon services, Wednesday night bible studies, Saturday afternoon rehearsals, biblical confessions and the prayers of others were speaking up for me in a weak moment.

...and pray for one another, that you may be healed and restored. The heartfelt and persistent prayer of a righteous man (believer) can accomplish much [when put into action and made effective by God—it is dynamic and can have tremendous power]. - James 5:16, amplified.

The enemy doesn't really care about whom he is influencing. He just wants an able body. He will walk through any open door of opportunity including your thoughts if he is given access to that space. He figures if he has your mind then he has your future. For by your thoughts your actions become truths. Eventually you live out what your heart has trained you to believe. It is your acceptance speech to life. Your life is the platform by which you project the seeds that you have allowed to take root in your mind and heart. From there they are released in full bloom as you speak.

How effective are you if your mind is not operating at one hundred percent of the potential that God purposed it? No, you will never be perfect. However, you can totally surrender yourself to the Father. It is in surrendering that you become transparent and allow God to reveal your true identity. So many people are searching for the real them, walking around with veils over their faces and blinders over their eyes. Many have become disturbed by the questioning of their own identity as I have done on many occasions.

As I mentioned before, I began having an identity

crisis early on. There was always a hunger to please people. I can remember my mother sharing stories about me giving away my personal belongings just to have friends. I was about four or five years old when it became a practice. Still today I am unclear as to how this stronghold entered my life at such a young age. Most people assume that in order to experience such challenges one must be a product of a broken home or a dysfunctional family. That just wasn't my story. However, I did come to find out that when you recognize that people pleasing is just an outward display of internal battles, you open the door to freedom. The moment you release those issues to the Father you can then walk in freedom. You do have a choice. Don't drive yourself crazy.

Before we dig deeper let me give you a little history. My mother gave birth to me while still in high school at the age of 17. I even attended her graduation ceremony. My father was 22 at the time. Two years after my birth they married each other and are

> **"When you recognize that people pleasing is just an outward display of internal battles, you open the door to freedom."**

still married today. Both gave their lives to the Lord and provided a solid foundation for our household. My dad worked manual labor in North Carolina for a major tire company while also ministering as the church organist. As a child my mother returned to school to work as a Chiropractor's assistant and served the congregation by ushering them down the aisle of the church every Sunday morning (white dress, white nurse's shoes, a gold name badge and all).

I remained an only child for a little while. Eventually, my younger sister and brother were born into the family. The three of us were actively involved in school, extracurricular activities and church. I welcomed Jesus into my heart at the age of 12 in the same bedroom that I battled thoughts of inferiority. To the human eye my life was everything but horrible. So according to life standards I should have never experienced the mind battles that I was tortured with for most of my life. We were the picture perfect family.

During elementary school, at a time that I was the most vulnerable, I did experience sexual abuse outside of our home. I did not recognize it as such until I had my first pap smear as a young adult. The procedure unexpectedly triggered raw emotion. So I know in part why I experienced some of the challenges. However, I choose not to discuss the details of my experiences in this book. By age 14 I was casted for a role in a gospel stage play and toured for a short period. At the age of 17, I was part of my 2nd gospel group, singing on radio commercials and being featured as guests for concerts. Three great kids, summer vacations, actively involved parents... How could there be any dysfunction? How could the enemy gain access to an environment dedicated to the Lord? But as I would eventually learn the enemy doesn't like to sit on a seat of do nothing when you are hard at work. He likes to wreak havoc! In order to make it I had to be willing to fight to get to the next level in life. My personal agenda included plans of becoming the next biggest television journalist, making enough money to provide for my family and proving myself to myself.

So as the final phase of high school neared I prepped for my life as an adult. I was eager to go to college. I thought if I moved away my personal battles would not follow me. In my heart I wanted every negative characteristic that attached itself to me to just fall off. I hoped waving goodbye to my hometown meant so long struggles.

BeYouty

CHAPTER 2-COLLEGE GIRL

Eventually Charlotte, North Carolina would become my new home. I was enrolled as a full-time student at the University of North Carolina at Charlotte right before my eighteenth birthday. A country girl in a somewhat big city... It was my time to shine and make something of myself. My family was counting on me as the first to leave home and attend a four-year university. I wanted to become larger than Oprah Winfrey, producing award winning journalism pieces, eventually hosting my own talk show. Most children look forward to the day they can leave their parents' home and live as an adult. Nearing 18 years of age made me feel as though I could handle every problem life threw at me. I'm sure most of us thought that at one time or another as we transitioned into adulthood. I had traveled alone as a child on one occasion, but never anything like this. I was an adult who was being entrusted to be able to do adult things.

When I started college I had no personal means of transportation. However, I quickly connected with other students who did or utilized campus transportation. I settled into my new dorm room with my high school friend and started my first official semester of class.

During my time at the University (UNCC), I filled my time with activity after activity. I was a campus tour guide, contributor for the university newspaper, worked during the summers and slightly during the academic year. I also interned, started a campus evangelism team and participated in Campus Outreach. Singing was a joy in my younger days. So I even sang on the campus gospel choir and for a brief period with the church choir at a very popular church in Charlotte which is pastored by one of my favorite gospel singers. Eventually, I transitioned from there to another excellent ministry.

My father had been trying to guide me to the church since the start of my freshman year. However, he did not know the name of the ministry. He only knew that the church had a bowling alley in the basement. That was the only piece of the puzzle I was given.

How was I to find a church with a bowling alley in a city as large as Charlotte? But in true leader fashion God allowed me to connect with another college student who invited me to church for a Sunday morning service. On the way to service she informed me that they had a ministry for college students and would often use their bowling alley. My face lit up as she told me about it. God has a way of setting you up! During my time in Charlotte I became a member of that local ministry and also a part of the College Outreach ministry. It was there that I connected with some individuals who have become awesome men and women of God.

Attending service during the morning on Sunday, Sunday evening and mid-week, I was hearing the word of God pretty regularly. So as far as spiritual food is concerned I was literally sitting at a buffet. It was all you can eat! Although I was being fed the word of God I was still in a fight. There were days as a student when I would sit in my dorm room or apartment sobbing uncontrollably. I would fight depression when I had the strength. I noticed the more involved I became involved in ministry or the more I tapped into my destiny the more aggressive the enemy would press.

I recall sitting in service one evening. The pastor's wife was teaching as she did most Sunday evenings. I absolutely enjoyed hearing her share the gospel. She was the first woman that I encountered that actually made the devil run. I mean a good spiritual foot chase with the word of God… As far as I could see she didn't appear to be entrapped by the cares of the world. I wanted that so much for my own life that I was willing to get to church whenever I could.

I remember on a Sunday evening during the middle of service I began to experience an overwhelming feeling of heaviness. I scanned the congregation about three times to refocus my attention. That didn't work. So I began to say under my breath "In the name of Jesus, In the name of Jesus." About that time as I was looking ahead I envisioned myself standing up in the middle of service just screaming uncontrollably. I started to fidget a little as this was something I was only imagining. My heart was racing with no explanation. The vision seemed so real that I became concerned and nervous. I continued to pray in a low voice until I could reach the front of the church after service. I focused on the message up until the point in which I felt the attack. What I do recall is that everything I heard prior to this experience had to do with the enemy and his schemes. It's so typical of the devil to test your faith.

After the service concluded I was able to speak to an older sister in Christ that I had come to respect tremendously. She was over the College Outreach Ministry at the church and I trusted her enough to share this strange moment. Most people would probably think I was crazy or just start having an oil slinging contest! Shaking and nervous I told her what I envisioned. Being another great woman of faith she prayed for me immediately and gave me instructions to get to the altar. "You know what to do." "You heard that message right?" I responded "yes." Although I had not heard the message entirely I headed to the altar to cast my cares onto the Lord. The short span of word that I was able to grasp was enough for a seed to be planted. I recognized that the devil was pressing a little harder. Although, the enemy is cunning and works to deceive people he is also predictable. He pulls some of the same tricks over and over again. That Sunday evening the enemy was seeking to trigger what was familiar to me.

Just because you are a believer does not mean that the enemy places an exempt from attacks sign on your life. The enemy will come bringing some of the same tactics over and over again in an attempt to break you. If you are observant you will notice he typically will test you as soon as you hear the word of God (Mark 4:15). He wants to get rid of tools that God has designed to set you free. However, he (the enemy) should not prosper. You do have a choice in the matter.

Unfortunately, many of us have failed the same life tests on more than one occasion. I have done so myself too often. You may have had five jobs in your life and ended each one with the same results. You quit because you feel the manager never liked you, showed favoritism, or because you could not contend with your competitors. So you quit each job eventually regretting your decision. What about dating someone who does not have God's best interest for you at heart? Abusive relationships? Ever find yourself falling for the nicely dressed, eye appealing guys who treat you like trash? Maybe not... Those issues could be foreign to you. Well are you the person who flips out because the waitress or cashier messes up your order? Sometimes we are really manifesting those internal battles outwardly. Doing so covers up past hurts that unconsciously reappear without notice. Until they are identified and removed you may experience repeats in your life. Ask yourself this question. Am I a repeat offender?

Before we move on with this chapter, I want you to identify hurts from your past that are still in your heart today. How do they show up? Here you want to give specific ways that reveal that you are holding onto issues of the heart. For example, if you are easily angered, talk about what upsets you so easily? If you find yourself fighting depression or anxiety do you notice anything that may trigger negative feelings?

I have found myself harboring feelings for years thinking it was always the other person. Yes they often had their part to play in the situation. However, the truth is the guys who treated me like trash could have never done so had I not given them access. I allowed it to happen. At some point you would think that the effects of bad decision making would enlighten us as individuals.

However, many times people become accustomed to making wrong decisions in life. You can do it so much that you become desensitized to doing things God's way which is the kingdom way. You get involved with the wrong men so much that when the right one comes along you run him away because you haven't learned how to love or even allow yourself to be loved. You keep closing the door, shutting the right guy out without even knowing why. So you blame him all because you you're covering up that wound.

So much of what we give out to others has to do with the condition of our heart. You may have noticed that when you identified your hurts in the exercise. The enemy doesn't care about how he achieves his goal. He just wants to make it happen. So you better believe that he will try to use any available avenue to get to your heart including your emotions, identity, self-esteem or people within your inner circle.

> The thief comes only in order to steal, kill and destroy. I came that they may have and enjoy life, and have it in abundance [to the full, till it overflows] (John 10:10 Amplified).

> 1 Peter 5:8 says, "Be sober, be vigilant; because your adversary the devil, as a roaring lion, walketh about, seeking whom he may devour (King James)."

The key is recognizing the test as soon as it is placed before you. The next time you get to the drive thru and "Catherine the cashier" hands you a bag short of what you ordered ask yourself, "is this my test." At the point that you notice the food is missing I know you are thinking that it is an inconvenience because you are planning to get some quality time in with your friends and instead you are now running late. In actuality Catherine is not to blame for every mishap of your day. All you wanted to do was grab a quick meal for the kids and drop them off at your parents' house. But before you ever had the opportunity to do that, the fish jumped out of the fishbowl onto the floor at home. You had a rough day at work. The kids hadn't done their chores when you arrived home. Someone forgot to pay the electric bill and you received the past due automated call on your way home. I know, been there done that!

But here is what we have to remind ourselves. If it were not possible to maintain our cool then God would not have told us to do it. My God is a God that will not lie. His word is true. You can either set yourself up for a blessing by extending some mercy or you can choose to do otherwise. If you choose the latter remember you will receive the same test soon. However, the fire may be a little hotter than before.

But let's say you do opt to give the cashier a piece of your mind for adding sorrow to your day. What do you prove to the cashier? What are you proving to yourself? If you give yourself a thorough evaluation you may get a rude awakening. Instead of pinpointing the cashier for causing your issue you may notice that you need to some develop compassion, love, grace or just exert some self-control. We are given the opportunity to learn more than we think.

BeYouty

CHAPTER 3-STUDY GUIDE

My greatest challenges came when I became a wife and mother. I thought I could really see myself clearly in a mirror prior to that season in life. However, I found that my true colors show more in my interaction with people, especially those in my home. You may be wondering why. I don't get paid to be a wife or a mother. So I'm not pressed by a paycheck. If you act a fool at work you run the risk of hitting the door, with a box in hand or in some cases, in the mail.

However, if you come out of the box at home on Tuesday, on Wednesday you still expect to have the same address. Well.... maybe. Maybe not. But you get the point. Your spouse and children may be walking around looking at you with the side eye. They're just not going to let you go so easily. Home is the place most of us expect to be able to let our guard down a bit. However, it's also the place where you may receive the most pressure.

> "Be angry and do not sin, Ephesians 4:26 (NKJV)".

> "Go ahead and be angry. You do well to be angry – but don't use your anger for revenge (MSG)."

I do not believe that God places tests in your life or brings problems. However, he will give you the tools necessary to pass the test. It is your job to educate yourself through the word of God. That is your greatest resource. If anger is your issue go to the word of God and see what He has to say about it. He cares so much about you that he doesn't want to see you walking around like a mad woman. If you are fornicating and want to know why it's wrong, go to the word of God for the answer. It takes work, no different than studying for an exam in school or a driving test. Trust me; you will have every opportunity to prove yourself.

> "Study and do your best to present yourself to God approved, a workman [tested by trial] who has no reason to be ashamed, accurately handling and skillfully teaching the word of truth (2 Timothy 2:15 Amplified)."

God's word is a study guide. It's a cheat sheet. And by all means don't forget the guidance of the Holy Spirit. Jesus even left us a comforter and He has a job.

> "But the Comforter, which is the Holy Ghost, whom the Father will send in my name, he shall teach you all things, and bring all things to your remembrance, whatsoever I have said unto you (John 14:26 KJV)."

"According to the word of God the Holy Spirit is the greatest teacher."

I know most people believe that experience is the best teacher. I have not found that to be true. Experience is great in its proper place of course. But experience is definitely not the best teacher as it relates to spiritual growth and guidance. According to the word of God the Holy Spirit is the greatest teacher. Before you try to rebuke me just reference the scripture above. That's not to say that you can never gain insight or learn from the things we experience on this earth. However, if experience were the best teacher we would have less people who become bitter and hateful after they encounter hurt. It takes wisdom to go through one of life's toughest moments, walk away still intact and apply what you learned in the next chapter of your life. Imagine if we actually allowed ourselves to be guided by the Holy Spirit in every conversation with our spouse.

I can hear someone now! "If Jesus were down here on this earth sitting beside me my husband still wouldn't change." I get it! But you can't change your spouse anyway. However, you do have the ability to surrender your own ways to the Lord and win him or her over just by being a representative of Jesus Christ. There have been days when I am straight up in my flesh and would rather give my husband a piece of my mind instead of allowing the peace of God to flow through my mind. That's not taking heed to the word of God. That's not allowing the Holy Spirit to do His part. So what happens? I get the same test repeatedly, giving me the opportunity to just shut my lovely lips. I know many people may ask, well what about him? You can't control him. Your job is to work on you with the help of the Lord.

For most of my marriage I was always reactive. We started out pretty rocky as you will come to know in the chapters to follow. However, when my heart was battered I had a tendency to fight back with my mouth. It's so much easier to feel like you are in control when you try to respond with hurt in an attempt to hurt someone else. I have found the more I practice choosing my words wisely the more those words become a part of who I am.

While I have not arrived I have made progress. Whew, thank you Jesus! I'm sure there are moments when my husband says the same thing under his breath. He's probably had several "come to Jesus meetings" concerning me. Sometimes it takes starving your flesh to death! No, I don't mean literally going on a hunger strike. I mean actually denying the natural man its' selfish ways. We are fighting the fight of faith.

BeYouty

CHAPTER 4-EXIT HERE

Life is filled with u-turns and wrong exits. We venture out on this journey called life trying to get to our destination. Maybe some of you are at a point of trying to figure this thing out right now. If you keep your ears open God will speak. Just be willing to listen.

By age 21 I graduated from school with a bachelor's degree and began a paid internship at a local television station in Charlotte. Within about two months I was offered my first on air position as a news reporter at a small cable operated station in Cartersville, Georgia. I was ecstatic! I found my new apartment online within weeks of finding out that I had secured a job. My parents, grandfather (who has since graduated to heaven) and I loaded the U-Haul and drove 6 hours to a place I had never even visited. It was night when we arrived and the apartment office was closed. I had to knock on the door of the office manager to get the key to my apartment. Small town perks... My parents were a little spooked at the idea of having to leave me in a place of the unknown. But they did it and I'm sure it was with much prayer.

It was in my nature to get connected to a church. So with the assistance of my former pastor in Charlotte I immediately began attending services a few cities away, but still in the Metro Atlanta area. I would go to service, hear the word of God but by the end of the week I felt lonely. Sometimes that's just a stirring of the flesh for some attention. This feeling of loneliness caused me to become a repeat offender in another area. Instead of seeking the Lord to bring me fulfillment I searched for it in people. And since I didn't choose to obey God on several occasions I found myself trying to figure life out once again. I'll explain how a little later.

So there I was a young adult in Metropolitan

Atlanta working on my full-time job in my career field. I was confident that I could handle my job as a reporter. Unfortunately, I was not 100 percent secure with was my appearance. I questioned the length of my hair, quality of my clothes and my thin frame. I made it to television and was still questioning God's blessings. The enemy was out to sabotage my mind.

Here is what is so profound. No one was bombarding me with negativity. Not one person in my circle brought attention to the way I looked, dressed or carried myself. My family and friends were all really excited that I was on air living out my dream of being a news reporter. If anyone ever thought otherwise they never said anything to me directly. So my thoughts were all self-inflicted. You can't expect to hear the word of God and just sit on it twiddling your thumbs. It's like depositing millions of dollars into your bank account while complaining that you are broke. At some point you have to make a withdrawal to reap the benefits.

Now as an adult I was still feeling some of those negative defeated insecurities from my childhood. I felt inferior in some cases and there were too many access points to my spirit. So yes some of the things that I experienced in my childhood stuck with me. However, we have to learn to tighten up our bootstraps or stand up straight in our stilettos and walk forward in faith. You are not your past! You are not defined by others labels. You are who the word of God says you are and nothing less!

So I put on my face for the camera, kept working and did my job. Unfortunately, I didn't believe everything God said about me. By then I'd just learned how to act like I did. I was well versed in the fine art of masking.

My time as an on air reporter and anchor was short lived. I submitted my resignation about one year later. So at age 23, I left my job as a rookie news reporter to become a teacher at a private Christian school in the same state. I was youthful and eager to help pour out my heart to a classroom full of 5 and 6-year-old children. I taught for nearly one academic school year and loved seeing the precious faces of the children in my classroom each day. At that time I prided myself in so many things to include saving myself for marriage. It's almost unheard of to come in contact with a 23-year-old virgin these days. But it is absolutely possible. Several women are living examples.

I came in the door a virgin and left broken and pregnant out of wedlock. That one thing that I held so close to my heart was released. How does that happen to the church girl? Surely being a single parent was not part of my personal agenda.

One day while still working as a reporter I received a knock on my door that would literally change my life. I had just gotten in from work and started to unwind when I heard that knock at the door. When I answered there appeared a guy, standing about 6'3 or so. He said he lived in the neighborhood. As my grandmother says, I didn't know the guy from the man in the moon. He said he had noticed me arriving home on a few occasions. We chatted a little that day. By the end of the conversation which was held as I stood behind my screen door, he asked me out to a movie. I thought, "hey why not?" So I obliged him. I thought maybe this is the guy for me or maybe not. I was surely going to find out. High expectations from such an empty place...

We hung out for some time and eventually became sexually intimate. My virginity was out of the door within a short period of time. I remember calling one of my closest friends who was in law school at the time. I had to tell her about my horrible decision to give myself to a man of whose last name I did not bare. She encouraged me and I committed to do better. Then next week I recommitted...then the next week....and so on.

It was the companionship that I desired. I had someone to watch movies with on occasion. We talked after a long days of work. But he didn't have high regard for me as a woman. And I put up with it. Jesus Christ wasn't even on the tip of his tongue. I fooled myself into thinking that I was stronger than he was spiritually. So I thought that I could handle the pressure of being alone with a man. As hungry as I was for affection and attention I should have barricaded the doors! But no I thought maybe I would be the person to get him on the straight and narrow. Maybe he would have a come to Jesus meeting on my watch. Wrong! Single ladies please do not go into dating as a missionary with your super

> **"Single ladies please do not go into dating as a missionary, with your super salvation cape on trying to rescue him from his sins."**

salvation cape on, trying to rescue him from his sins. That is a red flag that alerts you of your attempt to fill a void. No natural satisfaction can heal a spiritual wound. Allow the Lord to cleanse his heart and mind. That's not your job. You are not the Holy Ghost. Your potential mate will not come to you in a perfect state. But you should at least have the peace of God when he arrives. For starters let the man at least have a relationship with the Lord. If not, may I encourage you to run the other way or in my best bible verbiage, "Turn the other cheek."

As I continued my job as a teacher my daily commute was becoming very costly financially. So I found an apartment a little closer to my job right outside of Atlanta. I connected with new friends and moved on. I had not spoken to the guy that I was sexually involved with for a few months or so. That is until I reached Christmas break. Those two weeks off as a teacher can be your saving grace when you are living right. However, when you are catering to your flesh, those two weeks can be a thorn in your side. I was battling with my flesh.

I remember practically calling all of my friends to just have a conversation and prevent myself from making "the phone call." I mean I pulled out all of my old address books. No one was available. I was in repeat offender territory again. So I picked up the phone and I called "him." I had disconnected from "him" because I knew he didn't have a relationship with the Lord and meant me no good. I was vying for attention from someone...anyone. During that phone call I received a crazy offer! "Why don't you come up here to see me?"

So that night I drove 30 minutes to get to him. There are probably thousands, maybe millions of women who make that same drive at some point. I battled within myself the entire drive. I felt as though God were mentally slowing the trip down so that I could get off on the next exit and head the opposite way on the highway.

Have you ever had a moment in your life that seemed like it was going in slow motion? I'm raising both hands and feet on this one. God was making a way of escape for me. But I didn't listen. My spirit tried to kick in! "This is wrong!" "I should go home, watch re-runs of "Amen" or "227" and eat butter pecan ice cream." "It's late at night." Why am I doing this?" I kept driving until I got to his apartment. My flesh won that night. Needless to say we were intimate and I felt guilty and dirty as I had every other time we had sex. I thought I would stay overnight and just go home in the morning. Instead I heard the words, "you know you have to leave right? She may be here tonight." I'm sure I looked as dumb as I felt in that moment. I don't even know if in that moment I knew there was a "she." I thought I was "she."

I got dressed and left feeling embarrassed and powerless. Of course that was a cold winter drive home not to add the drive home was just as lonely as the trip going. I want to take a moment right now to tell every single woman who may get that call tonight, DON'T GO! It is not worth the drive honey! Pray through your struggle. And if you must drive, go straight to your female friend's house so that you can have some accountability. Drive to all night prayer, to you parents' house or drive yourself right into your closet and pray. Just don't go to see "him." You will be okay when the sun rises.

When I arrived home that night I showered, curled up in my bed and fell asleep. For the next few days I beat myself up over that decision. Over time I began to notice some sensitivity in my breast and then a missed cycle. Weeks later I found out I was pregnant with my first child. My only thoughts consisted of what everyone else would think about me being a Christian who was pregnant, not to mention I was working at a Christian school. My decision could cost me my job.

For the next several months I felt as though I had a sign that read "Heathen" across my forehead. Each day I would go to work representing God before these five and six-year-old children. That was one of the toughest things I had to do. And it was all because of the guilt and shame that I carried.

I remember one day as I stood in front of my class teaching, one of my students raised her hand. As usual I stopped my lesson and acknowledged her. She looked at my stomach and said "Ms. Street you look like you're pregnant." As all of the kids stared at my stomach I felt what seemed like my heart falling to the ground. My response, "oh do I." She said, "yeah you do." I had one of the most intelligent kindergarten classes. So I knew there was the possibility that they would find out considering I was about five months pregnant at that time. By then I thought I would have gotten past the sin that I had committed. I was making myself pay for it. In reality I repented the night that my child was conceived. God forgave me at that moment.

However, I allowed some cruel words and the opinions of others to haunt me. I heard everything from "you're damaged goods" to "no one is going to marry you now!" I understand now that it was just so unexpected that no one knew what to do with the information. I have a relative who believed for years that I had been raped. That's how out of character my family thought it was for me. Most people were very supportive.

I recall calling my parents to let them know that I was pregnant. I was so fearful of what they would think of me, especially my dad. My heart was beating so fast as I dialed their number! My mom answered the phone. Then my lips finally parted. "I'm pregnant." My mother responded as though she didn't hear me. "What did you say?" I said it again. "I'm pregnant." My mother passed the phone to my dad probably from shock. What my father said to me that day changed my thoughts. He said, "well as long as you got things right with God it's okay. You've just got to make sure that you pray over the baby. It will be alright." That was the greatest feeling of relief that I'd ever experienced. The burden was lifted and I felt so much lighter. This meant so much coming from the man I had watched living a life committed to God. He was a church musician and still is to this day. He is a hard worker and provider of his home. I have never known of anything outside of that. So for him to offer that reassurance gave me the okay to move on.

That year I had to return home due to conflict of interest at my job and the unsuccessful attempts at finding a new job. My greatest support was back in North Carolina where I could be surrounded by a loving family. Although I was no longer in Georgia I still received a great deal of support from former coworkers and friends who were aware of "my situation."

I am so appreciative of the circle of love years later. There is no way that I would have been able to stand without those individuals being in place. I know now that they were there by the grace of God. Unfortunately, acting in disobedience took me down a different path than I ever intended to go. Instead of building myself up spiritually I fed my flesh. I looked for fulfillment in a man who was not supposed to be a part of my story. Thank God for makeovers!

BeYouty

CHAPTER 5-THE RESCUE

I always looked forward to birthing a child. However, I never intended to be a single parent. As I mentioned before that was not a part of my life story, at least not the one I'd planned for myself. So just three years after graduating from college I was back at home with no job which meant no income and another mouth to feed.

Like most women I learned to make due and used what I had to get what I wanted. So I was blessed with opportunity to do some side work for a relative until I was able to land a solid job. From there I worked a couple of customer service jobs connecting with all the wrong men yet again. Seeking love and affection I surrendered my body for the pleasure of men. I don't think at any point that I believed any of the relationships or sexships could lead to marriage.

It's amazing how often we set standards for ourselves that we allow to be kicked down. We often do so out of desperation for attention or a desire to be loved. In 2005 I began a relationship with a guy who was about 14 years older than me. He owned his own home, had a couple of cars and had a couple of children from a previous relationship. I met him over the telephone. Who does that?!?! Me, yes this sister right here. It happens more than you know. Although now with the advancement of technology we now have dating network sites that make connections for you. Please know that if this is the direction you chose to go I am not condemning you. It was a dead end for me.

I enjoyed the company of this new guy and I guess he enjoyed mine. By then my daughter was about 3 years old. In my gut, I just had a feeling that he was always up to no good. That was that still small voice that everyone talks about. It's called the Holy Spirit. It had become my nature to not even listen by that point. I had some form of selective hearing. If you have it get rid of it.

This relationship still seemed a little different than others. He lived in another state and we only saw each other here and there. He said all of the right things to me. He used all of the right terms of endearment. And I loved the way he said my name. It gave me goosebumps, kind of how you feel when you get a nice gift that is packaged just right. However, when you open it you're immediately thinking of ways you can re-gift it. I felt special and unwanted all at the same time.

This guy even spoke about marrying me. One night as we talked on the telephone he told me how much he wanted me to be his wife. Reflecting back I don't think he ever told me that he loved me one time in the relationship. Red flag! He said things like "you know I care for you, right!" If I could just insert a side eye right there... However, he wanted me to be his wife. I had feelings for him, but I wasn't romantically in love with the guy. At that point I was tired of being a participant in everyone's wedding. DOG ON IT, I wanted my own day, my own wedding dress with my own bridal party! If I had to buy one more dress or attend another wedding ceremony or reception and my name wasn't on the front of the program I was going to scream!

The guy even told me that he already had a wedding ring for me. He even had the nerve to follow that up by telling me that he kept his ex-wife's wedding set. I know! The red flag was on fire at that point!!! The banner was waved and flown in the sky. However, I chose to ignore it (selective hearing). I was still considering wearing his last name. I was in love with the idea of having a man to come home to, someone to hold me and comfort me when I needed it, a nice home in a beautiful neighborhood and two car garage. It seemed like a pretty nice deal to me. I never considered what I would have to give up in exchange for a new last name.

Ladies, there is a difference between desiring a mate and being desperate for a mate. Desperation can potentially bring you a monster. Remain in the will of God if you desire to be married. Let the Father bring you the right man of God. Wait on Him!

One night I attended a women's conference with a beautiful friend of mine who now supports her husband as a pastor. We went expecting to receive whatever the Lord had to say through Pastor Nancy Dufresne. I had heard of her before and sat with great anticipation not knowing what the Lord would do.

That night she preached and began closing the service. She paced the floor and said something to this effect. "The Lord wants to say something to someone here. So I can't close the service out until he speaks." I know the entire church could hear my heart beating. I just knew the Lord was telling Pastor Dufresene that I had fornicated with my significant other not too long ago and that I needed to be set free and delivered. Don't we all go through that? We live in sin or keeping walking back into sin and fear being called out by those who are fully committed to the Lord. So my heart is beating a mile a minute and there is complete silence in the sanctuary.

The room is packed from wall to wall. I mean every seat is literally filled in the church at least from what I could see. I was seated about 10 seats from the front on the far-right section of the sanctuary, maybe the third person from the aisle on the row. Pastor Nancy was pacing the floor on the far-left section of the sanctuary. She began walking to the right, her left. My heartbeat rate increased! She came closer and closer. "Oh my Jesus, she is coming to me! Lord, I repent right now for fornicating with that man. I know it wasn't right. But please don't call me out in front of all these women." I looked up and she was right at my row.

She looked at me as said, "You, can I talk to you for a minute?" I could have passed slam out right there in the middle of the service. And I don't mean slain in the spirit! Certainly I wasn't going to tell this woman of God who came all the way from California that I didn't want to hear a word from the Lord. So I stood up and entered the aisle where she stood. She grabbed both of my hands very gently and said, "You know the Lord loves you right?" I said, "Yes." She said something like this, "He loves you so much that He wants to send you a husband, a man of God. But if you marry the one that you're with now you will regret it for the rest of your life." I broke down crying! How could it be that a woman that I had never met before could come all the way from California to minister at a women's conference to hundreds of women and God has a specific and in season word for Shanita?

In that moment I was reminded of God's faithfulness and love towards me. He loved me so much that he sent someone who He knew would knock some sense into me. That was the most lovely gut punch I had ever encountered. This was the first time that I had experienced a total stranger being used by God to speak to a specific situation in my life. I had received general prophecies before. But never anything like this!

When the Father stops your show to bring you back to reality you know He is a loving God. So Pastor Dufresne prayed with me and I returned to my seat knowing exactly what needed to take place next. I ended the relationship within days.

Letting go is not always an easy process. If you want to keep the enemy at bay you must learn to apply the word of God in your life. After ending the relationship I recognized the significance of building a circle of friends who had common spiritual goals. They are the individuals who will pray for you in weak moments. As a believer when you go through turmoil in your life you do not need people to speak death and doom over your life. You don't need sugar coating

Sally trying to hide the truth from you. Give me tell it like it is Tonya. We all have that friend who is great enough to comfort you when you are going through. But she is real enough to call your bluff. Yes, that kind of friend!

BeYouty

CHAPTER 6-NOT AGAIN!

I was making spiritual progress and became more focused on God than I had been in years. On occasion I would call up some of the singles in my new church and set up fellowships. Life seemed to have taken a turn for the better. I was determined to keep my body under lock and key until my husband made his debut. Within three months of making that committed I was on my way to lunch with some of my single sisters and brothers when my then friend held a conversation as a passenger in my car. She giggled and chatted with the person on the phone. It was that last chuckle that would lead me into my next season. She looked at me and said "I don't have any single friends for you. Wait, yes I do. She's right here! Here it's my Uncle Antwan." Some people would call it a Holy Ghost hookup. She handed me her cell phone. After a very brief talk with Antwan we agreed to speak again.

Needless to say we began dating within a short time. He was two hours away in another state. So we saw each other about once a month but spoke every day. He was a father of two, worked hard and was actively involved in ministry. He loved music and so did I. At the time he spent much of his time writing, as he did some Christian rapping in his spare time. We spent hours talking about our love for Jesus Christ and our life experiences.

He would fall asleep on the phone trying to impress me with talk even though he had just worked a 12-hour shift at work. At the time I really didn't put much thought into him falling asleep during out conversation. I would let him know that I was ending the call once he caught himself sleeping. There are so many silly things we do when we are dating. They're sweet and innocent at that moment. Not much else really matters at the time.

Sex was something that wasn't on either one of our

radars when we began dating. But as we spent longer hours with each other we would put those principles to the side for the sake of pleasure.

When you do something over and over it becomes habit. Some of those habits are easier to break than others. We have a stronger will and desire to live out some principles over others. But it's a choice. Early on we both saw the potential of marriage but desired the benefits more. We allowed our perception of things to supersede God's plans. So we pushed the envelope more and more each time we were alone with each other. So by January of the next year I was pregnant again out of wedlock but this time by a believer. We were two believers who knew that God would give us the desires of their hearts but were too impatient to wait.

There are times in life when we change our Holy Ghost hookups into fleshly fellowships. Your feelings, emotions and intellect can speak over your spirit man if allowed. God is not the author of confusion. He covers a multitude of sin. But He is not your cover up when you need a cop out. When we make dumb decisions they're just dumb decisions. Give credit where credit is due even if it's wrong and the finger is pointing back at you.

It is absolutely the will of God for children to be born. However, we do not please Him in the act of fornication. Antwan and I were both willing to acknowledge our wrongdoings and repent to God. So according to the word of God we were forgiven. But condemnation was heavy. I was afraid of what everyone would say about the Christian girl who was pregnant again.

I mean how many chances would I get before people started to doubt who I really was as a believer? A month or two later Antwan proposed. I remember sitting on my grandmother's living room couch talking to Antwan when he asked about nail polish and polishing my nails. I recall thinking, "what is he talking about?" He then got down on one knee, probably as nervous as ever and asked me to marry him. It wasn't the most romantic proposal but I said yes.

It wouldn't take long before I began to have doubts about whether I was making the right decision. I had a conversation with his then pastor's wife. That was a conversation I will never forget. I shared some concerns I had about our relationship potential. The question she posed would play in my mind over and over each time Antwan and I had heated fellowship during the first 8 years of marriage. It is one I will never forget. Her response to my concerns was this; "if Antwan never makes any improvements or never makes any changes for the rest of his life can you love him as he is?"

That one question will preach independent of any other words concerning marriage. So if you are considering getting married ask yourself that question. Please understand it is not a negative question. It forces you to take a deeper look at yourself and your relationship with your potential mate. It's a real question! Just the thought of the answer hit me hard because up until that point I didn't quite understand the full commitment and covenant of marriage.

During my second pregnancy I became very sick and unable to work through the entire pregnancy. I lost my job during that time and had no additional income. So we stretched every penny possible. Antwan and I married a few months later, living apart for three months while my daughter completed the school year. I expected things to fall in place since I was righting my wrong. As I prepped for my new life as a married woman I had so much to consider.

BeYouty

CHAPTER 7–BLENDING

During the summer my daughter and I moved to South Carolina to be with my husband. We lived in a tiny two-bedroom apartment paying $450 a month for rent. The dynamics of our home are pretty complex and far from my experience with my own family. My husband has two children from previous relationships. So once married I became a bonus Mom. I have my daughter from a previous relationship. Together we have two children. Today, we have five children between the two of us. Jokingly, I sometimes refer to us as the "black Brady Bunch." Five kids with different sets of parents... No one in my family had been a part of a blended family at the time we were married. Let's just say I was the first to venture out.

As a teacher in Georgia I saw the blended family work successfully. A student of mine at the time was a product of a blended family. They seemed to have everything together from what I could tell. I'm sure it wasn't perfect as I was on the outside looking in. But both sets of parents came to parent-teacher conferences and had a rotating carpool. They even took a vacation together! Clearly, blended families could be friction free or kept to a minimum.

It didn't seem like a hard task to transition multiple children into one family. The truth is I had no idea until I was sitting in the middle of what felt like a whirlwind. Out of respect for our children I will not share details of the challenges in this book. If you are considering marrying someone with children or are currently parenting children in a blended family I encourage you to have a heart to heart with your spouse. Don't give any room for the enemy to come into your home.

I recommend discussing the following before marriage: blending the family, discipline, child support/visitation and communication between your spouse and parents outside of your home. That's just a start. But it will get you to a good place of understanding. Please do not leave any stone unturned. Flip every rock, stone and pebble over. Get it out in the open. I am no negative Nancy. So please don't think that it's not possible to have a successful blended family. The possibilities are endless! It just took my family years to work out some of the kinks. We still have a few here and there. However, I remain optimistic concerning the well-being of my blended family and yours too.

> "God will give you the grace to extend love in ways you may have never known."

Remember that blended families are constantly blending and becoming one. So never single your family out as being the "problem family." And please don't walk in condemnation when you experience challenges. Every family has their share. Blended families make up a large percentage of households today. Pray daily! God will give you the grace to extend love in ways you may have never known.

BeYouty

CHAPTER 8-A PRICE TO PAY

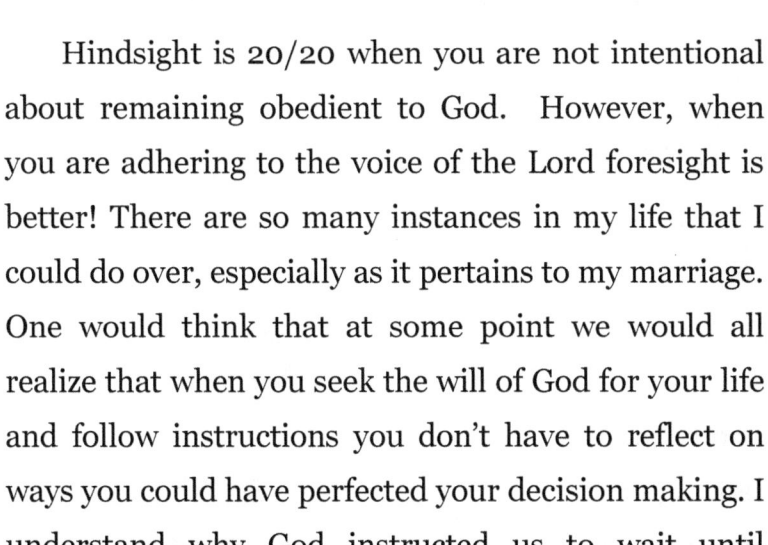

Hindsight is 20/20 when you are not intentional about remaining obedient to God. However, when you are adhering to the voice of the Lord foresight is better! There are so many instances in my life that I could do over, especially as it pertains to my marriage. One would think that at some point we would all realize that when you seek the will of God for your life and follow instructions you don't have to reflect on ways you could have perfected your decision making. I understand why God instructed us to wait until marriage to have sex. My husband and I have had the discussion on numerous occasions. There are so many risks that come along with fornication.

If you didn't save yourself for marriage I'm sure you could think of several. It opened the door for disappointments and heart breaks. The good news is I didn't have to stay in my disappointments. Neither do you! I have even better news. Your heart can be mended too.

For the first six years of my marriage I was miserable. I regretted getting married within the first year. Here's what I came to understand. I didn't marry my husband just for love. Remember, we were Christians at the time that I became pregnant. Since we were believers and we knew the word I figured it would be easier to put it into action as a couple. We cared about each other and wanted the best for our family. But we were not prepared for the reality of marriage at least not marriage within the dynamics of our household.

As a single woman I had listened to every tape and cd possible (podcasts and electronic devices were not as popular as they are today). So I thought I had pretty much mastered the art of submission in my mind. I'm not quite sure by what standards. However, by this time I gained confidence and didn't second guess myself as much. It was about that time that the enemy figured he would knock on the door of our apartment in Sumter, SC. Due to some insecurities my husband faced at the time, I was accused of cheating at about eight months pregnant. We were at a financial deficit and couldn't afford new clothes or to pay all of our bills with what little money we had. I hadn't experienced that much hardship in my life, even without a job as a single woman.

You can imagine the enemy was probably sitting back thinking he was about to have a field day with me. With all the right ingredients stewing in the pot he planned to turn up the heat. I was stuck with rotating a few shirts, shorts and pants for my daughter who was then four years old. Buying a new pair of shoes for her even seemed far-fetched. I was nearing my due date and made it priority to find a job. Day after day I would go to the library working on my resume and applying for jobs. I never received one call back from any of the companies. How could this happen to me? My life appeared to be spiraling out of control. My house was surely not a home.

Conversations between my husband and I were short and I was becoming frustrated and angry. I wondered did I just miss God and marry the wrong person. Before I knew it I became resentful towards my husband for everything that was happening. I recognized that I was merely putting up with things because I did not want to go through a divorce.

I recall one of several moments of desperation. It was one Sunday morning and the pastor extended an invitation to anyone who wanted prayer. I just wanted to feel something different in my marriage. I wanted to possess a genuine love regardless of how I felt I was being treated, regardless of the countless times that I felt alone. I wanted to be that Proverbs 31 woman that everyone labeled themselves.

Sadly, the Proverbs 31 woman is a banner than many people wear in public often laying it down in the closet with their shoes upon arriving home. So in my desperate and vulnerable moment I headed down the aisle instantly in the direction of a female altar minister. I thought, "Surely, she will understand me,

> "Sadly, the Proverbs 31 woman is a banner than many people wear in public often laying it down in the closet with the shoes upon arriving home."

have sympathy for me but pray this thing out of me." I told her that I didn't feel like I was in love with my husband and that I married him because I was pregnant. I was transparent and honest. She responded, "now you know no one does that, right? You had to love him to marry him." I agreed but with a hesitation in my heart. I was so embarrassed. How was she going to come into agreement with me while rejecting my truth? So as she was praying I was toiling within myself. Maybe I did love him and didn't even know it. I knew that I cared for him and l didn't hate him.

However, I no longer possessed that same feeling that I did when we dated and talked on the phone for hours on hand or when we would travel from state to state just see each other for a couple of days. I didn't feel protected or covered. I had come to the point of feeling unloved, uncared for and unprotected. I began to doubt his love for me as well. I often wondered how a man could say that he loved me so dearly, but yet make false accusations or fall asleep on me as I expressed my heart or accused me of the unthinkable.

It's really weird that something like falling asleep on the phone when you're dating can be cute. But when you get married and fall asleep on your spouse it can almost cause a war. I questioned how could the one person that I believed would hold my heart disrespect me or even allow other people to disrespect me? With every thought and almost every minute the anger and resentment grew.

September came around and I gave birth to my second baby girl Taylor. Now I was rotating outfits for two. By nature I am problem solver, leader and Mrs. Fix It. It was hard for me to sit back and watch my family go under and say absolutely nothing. My husband and I both sought out higher paying jobs in Charlotte, NC. We believed that would lead us to more opportunities as a family as well. However, everything there appeared to be a dead end. At the time there was very little opportunity in Sumter, SC and we needed a way out. My family had helped us out numerous times by then.

So I threw out the idea of moving back to North Carolina with my family until we got back on our feet. My husband was slightly hesitant, but eventually jumped on board. We loaded up my parent's truck, our cars and gave away anything that would not fit. Outside of coming to know some really good friends and family I was happy to escape the place that I'd come to call home.

By January 2009 we had arrived in Fayetteville, NC now residing with one of my family members. It felt good to be at home in a safe and secure place. My family became very instrumental in helping us to get back on good ground. Within a month I had landed a job starting at $40,000 which wasn't so bad. That was almost unheard of for an office job in Fayetteville at the time. My husband was hired quickly working in government in a neighboring county. Within months we were in our own place.

Things were on the up and up for the Rogers household. However, marital issues continued to grow along with the days. With the new doors of opportunity came jealousy and more accusations. We also began to experience greater challenges as a blended family. Prior to this time in my life I don't think I had ever talked to the Lord so much. I spoke to Him every day. However, the pressure prompted me to talk to him more often than usual. There were times when all I could do was just pray and cry out to the Lord. We argued so much that I could have written "The 5 Languages of Arguing."

Things had become so intense that we went to seek counsel from a couple that I have grown to love and respect. Ironically, the wife is the same friend that went to the women's conference with me when I got the revelation about my previous relationship.

Today they are wonderful pastors in North Carolina. We talked to them about our challenges and issues with each other. They offered some great advice. But we were so far gone by the time they finished counseling us that they said "you all are going to have to see someone else!" Now when two of the godliest and most loving people tell you something like that you know something is wrong! I can laugh about it today. However, it wasn't a laughing matter then and they knew it.

Meanwhile we were experiencing this horror story and my oldest natural daughter was being affected. She was about five years old at the time. Whether you know it or not children observe more than we think. We determine what types of seeds are sown into their ground. We can either make a conscious decision to give them something to look forward to in life or we can give them something to run away from in life. If our children hear us yelling and fussing at each other all the time they are more likely to duplicate those same actions in their own marriages. Demonstrating the love of God should be our preference. It is not always easy and takes work but it is worth it!

Still angered and resentful at times I made the decision to stick this thing out. A groundbreaking moment for me was when my husband finally took notice of how invisible I felt as a mother in our blended family. Again, I will not provide details. However, it became clear to him that I belonged in the position of his wife and not the invisible woman.

There are some issues that should never get to the level of argument. I was elated to know that I was free in that regards. However, we continued to argue. I wanted to state my point of view and he had moments of anger. I needed him to understand my heart. He wanted to walk out, never discussing any of the issues. I took it as rejection. He said he needed time. That was definitely not a good mix for me at that time. It was like pouring oil and water in the same bottle. They just didn't blend well.

As we continued to encounter the turmoil I was receiving calls from my ex approximately every 6 months. The first call came when I was pregnant in

Sumter, SC. Just in case you didn't know the devil is an opportunist. He takes time to observe and assumes position in what he feels is the weakest but best opportunity to peek his head through the door. He puts a lot of "what if's in your mind." It's your job to shut them down and cast them out. Had I been angry enough at the right time the invitations from my ex may have looked inviting. However, with each call that I received I made it clear that I was committed to God and my husband. Unfortunately, many have opened the door when the devil knocked. If that's you don't feel condemned. Make it right with the Lord and your spouse if you can.

Moving forward I received raise after raise and my husband was promoted. Somehow we were still at a deficit. So we moved back in with my family, praying it would be the last time that we would have to do so, but thankful for a place to stay. The arguments intensified.

There are things in life that we believe are the obvious. However, in a world so full of self it's not. When you face insecurities in your life you project that onto those closest to you. Eventually in a marriage if those insecurities are not dealt with they can become your spouse's insecurities. It would behoove you to rid yourself of any strongholds that come in the form of insecurity. If not, you will attempt to force your spouse to fill the void. No man or woman can fill that empty space. Words of encouragement and comfort can be offered. However, you must take the initiative to change it from the inside out through the loving guidance of the Lord.

Within time we looked to be making some progress in our relationship. It was always hard to tell. Some days we made jokes and had a date here or there. Other days we didn't speak at all. However, after much prayer and talking we decided to put our faith in action and move out again. We did just that! We moved into our new home. The kids had their own space, plenty of room in the backyard and a nice community.

We were attending a church that our children loved dearly. We joined and began going to service on a regular basis. I joined kicking and screaming (not really), just a little apprehensive. Okay, I was reluctant. However, my husband made it clear that he felt the Lord was leading us to that church. He said to me one day "that pastor really loves people. And the kids are getting taught." But I just didn't want to join. I thought, I didn't want to just hear contemporary Christian music every Sunday. I wanted to hear a diverse sound. I told my husband that all of the time. His response, "well you can listen to what you want when you get in the car."

Here's something hilarious. I was the person who told him about the church! I had visited for about one year as a single mother years ago. So it was all my fault anyway. You don't bring a guest to a table full of collard greens, cabbage, macaroni & cheese, baked chicken, meat loaf, chocolate cake, lemonade and sweet tea and tell them not to eat!

Sunday after Sunday I had to listen to music to the likings of Hillsong, Bethel and Jesus Culture. And there is absolutely nothing wrong with that sound. I actually have an appreciation of music. They were talking about the same God but a different sound than I wanted to hear at the time. I would literally sit in church and roll my eyes thinking "Lord can you send a little Fred Hammond, Marvin Sapp or somebody here and there?" My husband was as happy as a kid on Christmas with his first snow. The more the pastor said "I prayed for a church that looked like heaven" the more I felt a tug at my heart, not to mention there wasn't a day that I had attended the church that an usher or greeter didn't welcome us with a hug or a smile. I thought to myself "my Lord these are the happiest people on God's green and blue earth! Where are they from?!?!?" I had never seen anything like it. It was like they had swallowed a joy pill before each service. This church had so much Jesus to offer. We needed as many doses as we could get. There was a ministry area and small group for everything. It didn't matter if you loved Jesus and loved to knit. There was a place for you! Over time I grew into the ministry and began inviting everyone I knew.

Soon things began to get really nasty at home. Before long I found myself back in that dark and lonely place that I once knew as a child. Frustrated and tired my husband began to say things that turned the soil in my mind exposing the seeds that were once planted. Arguments became so intense that he would call me crazy, bi-polar and threaten me with the possibilities of being with other women. At one point he compared me to another woman and accused me of being jealous. Feeling insecure and broken I was hesitant and too embarrassed to share some of my deepest challenges with my husband as any woman would be. And since we had not submitted our own ways to the Lord on a continuous basis flesh took over.

On two separate but short occasions my husband left due to the tensions in our home. It was in that house that some of the biggest roots of insecurity grew. My life at that time was much like a Redwood tree. Redwoods are some of the tallest trees you will ever see. They have large roots that tie into clusters of other redwoods. They require water year-round and water themselves by utilizing the water trapped inside of their branches.

There were roots in my heart coming from every direction being entangled with my thought process, habits, family, dreams, career, marriage, finances, appearance and more. Because I wasn't consistent in rejecting what was unhealthy I allowed those roots to keep spreading. I became deeply depressed once again. My grandmother would often ask me "Shanita are you okay." Out of concern for her I would simply tell her yes. Thoughts of suicide were increasing. I never thought that I would face thoughts of suicide ever again. I had never felt so unwanted in my entire life.

No matter the accomplishments or achievements it was as though I was failing life all because of a few choice words that I allowed to become the root of my heart. I became very proficient at hiding myself from others. I wore a mask to church and work because I was too embarrassed to expose my reality to others. I would lie in my bed thinking of ways to take my life. The enemy had me so bound that I would play out scenes in my head over and over again of suicide. I remember on a few occasions riding with my husband on a busy street and considering jumping out of the truck into oncoming traffic so that he could witness my horrific death. I never imagined that the little girl who dreamed of having a beautiful marriage with a loving family would be back here again.

The enemy was setting up a trap of defeat. In spite of it all God still spoke to me. He spoke to me when I saw my children laughing, playing and sleeping. It was His reminder to let me know that I still had purpose. If nothing else, one of them was to raise my children and pour my heart out to them and those to come. Yes I had a purpose as a wife too. However, I couldn't see that through the hurt.

During this season of my life there was a tremendous amount of stress building up in my husband as well. I would watch him become frustrated feeling trapped by life's circumstances. So with my support he submitted his letter of resignation at his job. By that point I was making a little more and we could stay afloat until he found a new job which wasn't long. I felt an overwhelming sense of urgency to push myself a little harder.

Within a few months or so, he was able to secure a part-time job requesting as many hours as possible in an attempt to make up the difference financially. During that time we continued life as usual or at least we tried. Not long after I found out that I was pregnant only to learn that it was an ectopic pregnancy. We recovered from that and continued to work on us.

Desiring to see our blended family unite I planned a trip for the six of us over the summer. At the time I was about two or three months pregnant and also planning our family reunion. After the reunion we were off on our vacation with all four children. We went to Myrtle Beach, South Carolina and then headed to Sumter, South Carolina to spend time with family and friends. From there we headed to Orlando, Florida where we watched as our children exhausted themselves at an amusement park. Days later we visited The Martin Luther King Jr. Center in Atlanta, Georgia so that the kids would have educational experience while on vacation. It was like we were on tour. We crunched time due to my monthly prenatal check up on the Tuesday after our return.

After days away from home we arrived back in North Carolina in time to get the two oldest children on the plane to return home. Tuesday was appointment time. I was ready to get an update on baby Rogers. It had been about six months since we lost the last baby. So we were optimistic and excited! I remember lying on the table as the midwife placed the gel on my belly and began the ultrasound. She turned the screen around as if to keep me from seeing what she saw. She left the room and returned with the doctor. He glared at the screen. There was no heartbeat. One of them suggested getting some blood drawn. I was so baffled that I don't remember who said what at the time.

However, I went through further testing and returned for the results. My numbers weren't where they should be considering my term in the pregnancy. I was devastated! Two of my babies were gone in one year. My husband was so supportive. He nursed my mental and physical state of health making sure I took the time to recover. I questioned how this happened, not once but twice. I blamed myself for losing the babies. Maybe I stressed too much or maybe I overdid it that summer. I realize now that I may never know why. However, I do know that the tone of our home would not have been the healthiest for another child during that season of my life. I do not say that in selfishness. I say it because I no longer blame myself for losing my two babies. And do acknowledge the state of my home at the time. Although, the process hurt I just accept it as part of my story.

After a rough time and a little growth spiritually I was able to move on from some of the past hurts in my life. You can't really press forward when you are constantly looking back. Your life becomes a tug of war between the future and the past. One of them will win! The summer of 2010 we were notified that the owner of the home that we were renting decided to sell the property. So we were at it again, looking for a new place. I desired to buy a home so badly. However, we were not there yet. I didn't want to make any pressured decisions to purchase a house that I would not like.

So for a third time we moved in with my parents until we found a new place. This would be a test of all times! No longer would we be able to hide behind those fake faces pretending to be okay. If we had any time of heated fellowship they would now know. If we couldn't stand each other for a week and chose not to speak they would know. We were going to be exposed for who we really were. When we previously lived with another family member we could kind of keep things under the table. A couple of our heated fellowships were exposed there. But that would not work this time.

The New Year had started and as usual we began the Daniel Fast at church. As most people I too believed that 2011 would be my year of change. It was, but not necessarily in the greatest way. During January I began experiencing nausea and excruciating muscle pain. I would become winded as I cleaned the shower or sometimes as I vacuumed the floor. I knew I was out of shape since I had not worked out consistently in a while. However, this was a little different than the occasional huffing sound I would make if I had jogged a mile. It would last a day and then it was gone, just like that. So I ignored it and moved on. In this season of life I decided that I was going to write my first book. My husband offered to hold down the family obligations on specific nights. For a moment it looked as though we had turned over a new leaf. But when the leaf turned over the wind blew it right back on the other side. My husband and I argued so much that I never remembered what we were arguing about. I remember feeling alone and in a position that I didn't want to be in as a married woman.

When I was a little girl I remember rarely speaking up for myself. Boldness was absent from my life. I was void of all confidence. But for some reason I was bold as a lion when it came to defending myself against my husband. Anger became my megaphone. I spoke through it almost every day. When we argued I wanted him to feel every ounce of pain that he ever caused me. I wanted him to hear me loud and clear, never questioning me because after all I had to be right, so I thought. My words were as hurtful as the bite of a snapping turtle. All of the hurt from the false accusations, sharp words, comparisons to others and leaving me to feel alone were all balled up into a fire ball. Slowly, everything was unraveling.

The word divorce came up on a regular basis. I made it clear that we could go our separate ways. Although in my gut I wished I could blink my eyes and have a wonderful marriage. But I couldn't let my guard down and appear vulnerable to the person who had broken my heart. That was my attitude; protect what rightfully belongs to me. Many of us have felt that way. You may carry that same thought pattern right now. You have to ask yourself what is rightfully yours. If I was walking in the spirit and not the flesh I would have recognized that my marriage was rightfully mine. That's worth fighting for!

The more I felt unloved the more I disrespected my husband. I recall a day when I had an episode. That's how I have chosen to identify moments when I had nausea, muscle and joint pain. I needed to wash clothes but I was so sick that I could only sit on the couch. My husband came through marching with a hand full of clothes as if he had direct orders to wash them. He had a look of disgust on his face. In my heart I knew that he thought I was a fluke as it related to this battle. I couldn't understand why my family and friends were so supportive and my own husband refused to believe that anything was wrong. I began to battle in my mind, coming up with reasons as to why he was treating me this way. My initial thought was that he was no longer attracted to me and was cheating. Then I thought he was determined to push me away so that I would cheat. Eventually, I just came to the conclusion that he hated me. That is a pretty low place to reside in a marriage. However, after a discussing my concern he just let me know that he didn't think things were as serious as they looked.

I didn't know until marriage that I would look for my husband to confirm who God said I was. When he didn't I reacted in anger. When he did not meet my expectations I blamed him. We were both responsible for having our own expectations of what the other should be. He expected me to function like his mother; having breakfast, lunch and dinner ready, doing the chores, taking care of the kids, paying the bills and tending to the needs of each individual in the house. He also expected me to work a full-time job.

I expected him to be just like my father; tough as a nail, an extremely hard worker who had it all together for his family, always opening my doors, never walking ahead of me and helping me to cook the food we eat and clean the showers we bathed in and never allowing my automobile to go dirty.

Our expectations placed blinders on our minds never giving us the opportunity to extend grace. When I didn't cook a meal because I was tired from working a long shift and doing homework with the kids he was angry. When the bathroom looked like who did it and why and he was at home all day studying for a work-related test I was angry. Expectations have killed a lot of relationships. Everyone should have a standard of expectations. However, they should be clear before you get married. You should also create an atmosphere conducive to maintain the expectations. That applies to every form of relationship from marriage to parenting. Remember you are not marrying your parents clone.

Nevertheless, we made the commitment again to work at honoring our vows. We went to counseling and both shared out hearts remaining hopeful that things would improve. My husband became supportive during episodes and was my moral support during several doctor visits. For the next several years

I underwent testing for the pain and nausea. I also had a blood clot, a ruptured cyst and horrible migraine headaches. However, through it all I was determined to win! We were in a decent place in our marriage. We worked to forget the days of the old and concentrate on what was ahead.

Months later I still continued to have the episodes. We were believing God for healing and praying for a breakthrough when I decided to schedule an appointment with my OB/GYN due to some additional pain in my abdomen. My husband joined me. The symptoms were very similar to those experienced during pregnancy. I was having meltdowns just in regular conversations, stomach pains and restlessness.

One day my husband came into the room as I sat on the bed. I remember saying to him, "I don't know what's wrong with me." After saying that I just broke down in tears. I'm sure it was the most awkward moment for him, as I very rarely shed a tear. To eliminate the possibilities of pregnancy I took 3 tests on 3 different days. They were all negative. A couple of weeks later we arrived at the doctor's office and were escorted back by the nurse. We went through the details and challenges that I was experiencing. She then asked if I had taken a pregnancy test to which I replied yes. But she wanted to make sure. So I took another test and came back to the area at the nurse's desk. She left to get the results from the test. She came back around the corner and sat down in her chair. She wrote a note as we're waiting to hear that the test was negative. "Well Mrs. Rogers...you're pregnant! That's why you are experiencing some of those symptoms." My husband and I looked at each other laughing. He brushed his shoulders off and said "Happy Valentine's Day!" It was February 14, 2012 and my last child was conceived on my husband's birthday. We were soooooo ecstatic! God graced us again to conceive another child. We asked God for a healthy baby boy. He gave us just that!

BeYouty

CHAPTER 9-INSTRUCTION MANUAL

During my pregnancy we moved out of my parent's home into a new home in a great family community, less than four minutes from my parents. My parents have always been instrumental in our lives, especially as it relates to helping us with transporting the kids to and from school and extracurricular activities. And besides, what grandparent doesn't want to live close to their grandkids? It was a win-win for everyone!

This move was actually the calm before the storm. At the time of the move we were married a little over five years. I have heard multiple people say that the first five years of marriage are the toughest for most couples. As you now know our story was a little different than most. I love to hear of others stories about how they met, fell in love, got married, had children and are living a happy and healthy life. That life is attainable if you remain obedient to the will of God for your life.

> "Even when your world is shaking you must still believe! The storm may come. The winds may blow. But it will not take you out!"

Unfortunately, there are many of us who took the wrong turns too often. Like many couples we didn't have a traditional start to marriage. So if you are in what feels like a never-ending story of unhappiness. I want you to know that there is hope in what appears to be a hopeless situation. Even when your world is shaking you must still believe! The storm may come. The winds may blow. But it will not take you out! So stand strong.

Right after giving birth to my son Christian I was offered a work from home position with the same organization I had been employed by for nearly five years. While on maternity leave the organization had a massive layoff that affected people across the country. So the opportunity was right on time. I was making a decent amount of money at the time and loved the idea of being able to pick my kids up from the bus stop while on break or running to the kitchen to grab something to eat at my leisure. By then my husband had also received a promotion or two. As far as income goes we were heading in the right direction. We weren't rich by far. But we were a good place.

Again, I felt this could be an opportunity for a prettier picture of my life to be painted. Isn't it funny how we think every life issue will be repaired as a result of making more money? Yes a higher income can give you access to paying off debt, helping more people and gaining access to things you may need. However, it doesn't fix heart issues. And if you are not a good steward of money it may actually mask what is at the surface of your problems. That applies to anything in life.

During the year of 2013 I experienced several ups and downs. Truth be told, almost every year since the inception of my life at that point consisted of ups and downs. In my heart I knew that God wanted to do some things concerning ministry. It was apparent that He wanted me to connect with other women. The process by which that would happen was not always clear.

So I began to pray and seek His face concerning my purpose in life. Obviously, being a wife and mother were part of the plan. My heart felt there was more to the story. It wasn't coincidental as a child that God allowed me to befriend several girls who were abused, raped and misunderstood. The life stories of these girls and later women seemed to follow me throughout my life.

It was in listening to them that I realized that we are more alike than different. How many times have you had a conversation with someone with whom you shared the same struggles? We as women have a tendency to isolate ourselves from the rest of the pack because we fool ourselves into believing that no other woman has experienced the same heartache and pain that we live through. The problem is we concentrate so much on masking the hurt and putting on a show that we go through most our lives as broken wives, angry mothers and invisible friends.

When I realized that we all have so much in common the next step registered. I don't know about you but I would rather seek help and walk in the liberty of Jesus Christ than walk in misery for the rest of my life. That spring about 20 women met in my living room for breakfast, games and girl talk. We talked about our challenges. Most importantly we offered solutions. There is little to no benefit in sitting around and discussing the turmoil you have encountered with no efforts of solving the problem. I didn't want to have a male bashing session or a pity party. My heart's desire was to create a warm and inviting atmosphere for ladies to engage, encourage, enable, edify and exhale. That Saturday a piece of my purpose was birthed!

My heart was overwhelmed with joy! You have probably experienced it before at some point in life. If you have birthed a child then you know what I mean. Your body is stretched and pressed during the months and months of carrying the baby. You may have even experienced a time of growing weary. You just want to get the baby out because you have become physically exhausted. Delivery time draws near and then the baby is birthed! You forget all about the pain and stretching that your body endured.

Consider the feeling of earning a degree, watching your child graduate, being awarded employee of the month or even landing your first job. Those are major milestones! However, if you allow the feeling of being a failure to inhabit your heart and mind for too long you may battle your successes.

Each year I continued hosting women's workshops, a sleepover and various fellowships. Would you not know after God blessed me with several successful events I became doubtful? Pure foolishness right? But remember there is nothing new under the sun (Ecclesiastes 1:9).

I began to question my God-given abilities because I started focusing on what others were doing. I wasn't a preacher so why was I offering workshops? I didn't have a perfect marriage so how could I offer advice? Surely, I didn't have enough bling on and my skirt wasn't dragging a red carpet. I didn't have 500 people sharing my posts and events. Why would anyone listen to me? And not to mention as my husband and I began searching for a new home I was laid off from my job. We were no longer able to afford the higher rent. So forget looking for the new house to buy. In fact, we had to move into an apartment that was extremely smaller than the house we were living in at the time of my layoff. That meant no stainless-steel appliances, hardwood floors, no granite counter tops, no remote-controlled fans, little to no travel, no insurance, no backyard for the kids... I felt like everything caved in on me.

I know it sounds selfish. However, when you become accustomed to a way of living you expect to move forward not backwards. Had I looked at the downsizing from a different perspective I could have easily identified it as an opportunity for God to manifest the next level of blessings in my life. I've blogged and spoken on some of these very issues. How could I have fallen into this state of defeated thinking? Even as a Christian you must remind yourself of who God is in your time of tests. During your season of a drought God can bring a water supply. He is a well that will never run dry. So, don't ever doubt the power of God.

Still in my emotions at the time of the shift, I remember feeling so embarrassed and humiliated about having to downsize my life. I remember one day I began having a feeling of an anxiety attack. I was alone with my children. I ran into the room to keep them from seeing me. I told them to give me a few minutes alone. I sat on the floor of my bedroom of our new apartment overwhelmed and weeping. Within seconds my husband called. I answered in a shaky and weak voice. I told him that I was struggling with feeling like a failure. How could anyone receive anything from the girl who encouraged all of these women at one point and now she couldn't even sustain her own household.

He reminded me of the things he saw in me when we were dating which was about eight years ago at that time. He reminded me that our current state was going to change. It was in that moment that I realized that pride had been living at my address, right along with people pleasing. Isn't it crazy how the very thing that was familiar to you as a child can find its way back to your front door if you don't guard your heart? When you hear the knock at your heart make it a point to ask "who is it" before you open the door. If it's people pleasing just say, "no thank you. Low self-esteem doesn't live here anymore. So I don't want any!"

I had become so consumed with doing what I thought everyone else wanted me to do that I forgot who opened the doors of opportunity in the first place. My mouthpiece was going. So I never stopped giving

God credit for what was taking place. However, my heart chambers were empty. God was talking, but there was a shallow place. His voice was echoing from the emptiness. He was saying "Shanita I have so much more for you to give." I just couldn't hear Him. There's that selective hearing again. I was seeking His promise (the ultimate picture) without even knowing His full will (instructions to get to the promise) for my life.

You may have found yourself in that place at some point in life. You bring the new crib home inside of a box with a nice beautiful picture on the front. It has a matching changing table and dresser. However, you have only purchased one item, the baby crib. The mahogany wood looks great with the paint on the wall, just beautiful. You pull the pieces and screws out along with the instructions. You start looking at the box and attempting to assemble your masterpiece, never realizing that you placed the three pages of instructions behind you. Those are the very resources the manufacturer provided to you so that you can avoid the inconvenience of trying to figure it out on your own. Why do we create so much chaos in our lives?

I will never forget when I was a single mommy with my first child, my uncle came over to help assemble my baby girls new stroller. He sat struggling to get the wheels and bars to go together. Occasionally, he would pick the box up and look at it trying to duplicate what he saw. My great aunt from Rocky Mount, NC was with us at the time visiting my grandmother. She has since passed away but was very quick and clever with her mouthpiece. She responded, "well don't you think that would work a lot better if you just read the instructions?!?!?" Aunt Bertha B was 102 years old when she passed and about 89 when she made that comment. But she had a good point!

How often do we see the nice picture that God reveals to us and decide that we will just put things together without seeking His face to get His will for our lives? You see the picture of the new crib that you purchased. So you get excited! "Yesss!!! This is it! I'm about to do my thing! I'm going to put this crib together like nobody's business!" So you think you can handle the job independent of the instructions that came with the product. Yeah, you just lay those incredible black words on a white sheet of paper to the side. You have to be smarter than the manufacturer!

This is what we do in our own lives. God is like, "hello my child. If you follow my instructions for your life things will flow smoothly." Don't get so caught up in the vision that God has given you that you forget that He has the master plan. You're trying to put nails and screws in the wrong places. You have bars on the top that should be on the bottom. Imagine putting the crib together upside down.

That's what we look like when will live life without the guidance of our Father! Let God be God in your life. I cannot count the amount of times I have asked my children "why are you not following my instructions." I don't want to think about the numerous times God has probably asked the same. My grandmother always said "A hard head will make a soft behind." In other words, you learn things the hard way when you choose not to listen to the instructions given. Take heed!

This is also true as it relates to marriage. I wholeheartedly desired to have a relationship with my husband that emulated God's vision for our union. Fighting for man's approval seemed to be the story of my life. I just never thought that at over 30 years of age that I would still be fighting for it.

What I didn't recognize is that I was fighting for the wrong thing and didn't even realize it. Had I sought the approval of the Father I could have saved myself some misery. Obedience is so much better than sacrifice (1 Samuel 15:22)!

Eventually I did finally recognize the importance of submitting. And might I add at no time do you ever stop learning. Today my husband and I continue to work towards intentionally covering our marriage through the word of God. It's not always easy by far.

Together via social media we host "Fight for Your Marriage Month" to celebrate our month of marriage. We laugh a little more and talk about our plans for the future. We are still building and developing some areas in our marriage. Unlike the first several years of our marriage we tend to rely on God's word instead of our own selfish needs. In other words there's not as much heated fellowship these days. If you want God kind of results you have to make intention decisions to honor God with your life.

BeYouty

CHAPTER 10-PROBLEM SOLVER

The Problem

Today, I understand the importance of pursuing the will of God for my life. For years I chased God's promises without allowing Him to guide my footsteps. I trusted God outside of trusting myself. Thus being the reason I lived as a repeat offender. I knew very early on that that there was something that I was here to do outside of being a wife and mother. Those two are of course priority. However, I wasn't the only one who was aware of my potential. The devil knew as well. So it became a personal goal of his to try and alter my life by causing conflictive thoughts and outside influences. That is why I struggled with suicidal thoughts, anxiety, depression and insecurity. The reason we face insecurity is because of what is inside. Those insecurities are established through various avenues. When it's all said and done the enemy wants your purpose. He wants your happiness, your joy and your mind.

When you don't know who you are the enemy works endlessly to assign an identity to you. If he can he will use this culture, your thoughts or anything he possibly can to distract you from the will of God for your life. Why do you think we face so many battles in our homes as it relates to family? It is the one institution designed by God that is being tested in every way possible. Family is where we find support, love and comfort. But home is also a battlefield for many. Can you imagine how many real power couples would exist if we all demonstrated the power and love of Christ in our relationships every day and not just when we felt like it?

It wasn't until I asked God for instructions that I began to understand the path that I would take for fulfill my purpose. Our Father already knows our ending and it's not a plan of defeat. Unfortunately, like many of you there were so many ways that I sought to find my purpose. I was looking at who I was on the surface level. There were times I thought that if I changed my physical appearance I would change as a person. Plastic surgery was an overnight thought. But I was too afraid to consider it seriously. I thought if I married the perfect guy I would be complete. The perfect man doesn't exist. And neither does the perfect woman. Besides, your identity can never been found in a man. He can only affirm who you are. The truth is there is only one source for your identity. And that's Jesus Christ.

The Solution

What we need to examine is who we are underneath the make-up, without the filters and the layers of masks from the past. No longer do you need to be afraid to be you! We all have a past. We all have done things that we regret. Repent and move on. Do not give place to the enemy and allow who you were to prevent you from becoming who God wants you to be. Part of that process includes forgiving yourself. I learned a long time ago that forgiving yourself is sometimes harder than forgiving someone else. So if that's your challenge say this as often as you need to: "As act of my will and out of obedience to God I forgive myself." I learned that from a great woman of God while in college. It has helped me to forgive myself and others through this journey of healing.

Mind Battles

I know from personal experience that anxiety, depression, suicidal thoughts, insecurities are real. However, they do no define who you are. The word of God says this in Philippians 2:9-10.

"Wherefore God also hath highly exalted him, and given him a name which is above every name: That at the name of Jesus every knee should bow, of things in heaven, and things in earth, and things under the earth;"

Every name includes anxiety, depression, suicidal thoughts and insecurities! God is greater! The enemy tries to reconnect me with some of those same battles today. However, as soon as I recognize it I cast it down and it leaves (2 Corinthians 10:5). There is no other option! If you give the enemy an inch he's coming to try and take a foot. He tries to take over.

Remember that you are not alone even if you are physically by yourself. The enemy will attempt to convince you to believe that you have been forgotten. He desires to make a playground of your mind. He will jump from thought to thought until common thinking becomes exhausting. Don't get tired! Don't grow weary! Think on things that are true, honest, just, pure, lovely, good report and virtue and praise God (Philippians 4:8).

If you are thinking horrible thoughts recognize that they are inspired by the enemy. And anything that is birthed from him cannot be true, honest, just, pure, lovely, a good report or virtuous. If he is the Father of all lies it is not possible for him to speak truth. Know this, "Greater is He that is in you than he that is in the world." (1 John 4:4). By all means don't be afraid to get help. The word of God encourages counsel. So don't fool yourself into believing that people of God can't seek help from a counselor or therapist. That's a lie.

Why have I shared my story with you one may ask? I did it because I want you to know that it's not over! If you're 30 and are returning to college your life is not over! If you're 40 and unemployed your life is not over! If you're 50 and single your life is not over! If you're 60 and going through a divorce your life is not over! Bank account empty or full... Even if you have lost everything your life is not over! God can use anyone who desires to be used even when you feel like you have met your worse. He doesn't give up on you.

The only way you can lose is if you choose to do so. God can and He will restore what the locust stole.

"And I will restore to you the years that the locust hath eaten, the cankerworm, and the caterpillar, and the palmerworm, my great army which I sent among you (Joel 2:25 Amplified)"

> **"YOUR PURPOSE & VISION CANNOT BECOME A REALITY IF YOU NEVER GO TO THE STARTING LINE."**

Remember your purpose & vision cannot become a reality if you never go to the starting line. If I waited to be perfect before using my gifts I would be sitting for the duration of my life. Many of us have hidden our talents because we fear what people will say. I am not a perfect wife, mother, daughter, sister or friend. But neither is the person who may criticize me. Stop leaving your purpose in the laps of other people. They can't carry what you were meant to.

Are your thoughts about who you are holding you back? Make a conscious decision to not focus on all of your flaws and imperfections. That's just surface stuff! Beneath that are traits that need to be unveiled. You are bold, talented, beautiful, intelligent, joyful, ambitious, confident, gorgeous, witty, righteous and a child of God. Your gifts, talents and everything you could be are sitting waiting for you to take action. Bring that to the surface. Walk in your liberty and be free.

Action Step

How to Bring Beauty to the Surface?

R.A.L.L.Y.

Read your word daily!

Always Say What God Says About You!

Lock Your Gates! (Be careful of what you allow to come through your eyes and ears. They are your gates to your spirit and soul. What or who are you watching and listening to?)

Link Up With Likeminded People!

Yield Yourself to God & Pray!

BEYouty

30 DAILY AFFIRMATIONS

30 DAILY AFFIRMATIONS

Day 1- I can do all things through Christ that strengthens me (Philippians 4:13)

30 DAILY AFFIRMATIONS

Day 2- I am more than a conqueror (Romans 8:37).

30 DAILY AFFIRMATIONS

Day 3- I am fearfully and wonderfully made (Psalm 139:14)

30 DAILY AFFIRMATIONS

Day 4- I feel good about myself!

30 DAILY AFFIRMATIONS

Day 5- I am strong!

30 DAILY AFFIRMATIONS

Day 6- I am brilliant!

30 DAILY AFFIRMATIONS

Day 7- Today is a new day!

30 DAILY AFFIRMATIONS

Day 8- I love and accept myself.

30 DAILY AFFIRMATIONS

Day 9- Today is already a good day.

30 DAILY AFFIRMATIONS

Day 10- I am not my past.

30 DAILY AFFIRMATIONS

Day 11- I am brave.

30 DAILY AFFIRMATIONS

Day 12- I have gifts and talents.

30 DAILY AFFIRMATIONS

Day 13- I am beautiful.

30 DAILY AFFIRMATIONS

Day 14 - Regardless of the outcome I am a winner.

30 DAILY AFFIRMATIONS

Day 15- My confidence is in you Lord.

30 DAILY AFFIRMATIONS

Day 16 - I am valuable.

30 DAILY AFFIRMATIONS

Day 17 - I am loved.

30 DAILY AFFIRMATIONS

Day 18 - I am me and that's okay.

30 DAILY AFFIRMATIONS

Day 19 - I aim to please God.

30 DAILY AFFIRMATIONS

Day 20 - I am unique.

30 DAILY AFFIRMATIONS

Day 21 - My body is beautiful.

30 DAILY AFFIRMATIONS

Day 22 - I am a chosen generation, a royal priesthood, a holy nation and a peculiar people (1 Peter 2:9)

30 DAILY AFFIRMATIONS

Day 23 - I am who I am because of who you are Lord.

30 DAILY AFFIRMATIONS

Day 24 – Goodness and mercy are always following me!

30 DAILY AFFIRMATIONS

Day 25 – I exist because I have purpose.

30 DAILY AFFIRMATIONS

Day 26 – I reject thoughts that are not pure and honest.

30 DAILY AFFIRMATIONS

Day 27 – I do not walk in condemnation!

30 DAILY AFFIRMATIONS

Day 28 – I have a stable mind.

30 DAILY AFFIRMATIONS

Day 29 – I am an individual. There is no one who is exactly like me. That's how much the Father loves me.

30 DAILY AFFIRMATIONS

Day 30 – I am teachable and open to the guidance of the Holy Spirit.

BeYouty

Prayer

God I submit my ways to You. Help me to see myself through your eyes. Help me to become aware of anything that does not represent you. I believe that according to your word I have been delivered from the hands of the enemy. I denounce all plans to destroy your purpose and plan for my life. I recognize the schemes designed to entrap my thoughts. Therefore, I cast down imaginations and anything that attempts to exalt itself against your knowledge. I bring it into captivity through the power of the Holy Spirit. I cast my cares on You. Because of your son Jesus Christ I am free and free indeed. No weapon formed against me shall prosper. I thank you for protecting my mind from all hurt, harm and danger. Expose every tactic that comes to attempt to take my joy and peace. You have given me authority over my mind. So I speak peace, joy, happiness and stability. You are exalted Father! I rest in and rely on you. I will trust you for all of my days in Jesus name. Amen.

BeYouty

ABOUT THE AUTHOR

Shanita Rogers is a wife and mother in a blended family of seven. She is a former reporter who has written for several online magazines. One of her passions is seeing others living a life of purpose and freedom. Shanita now works in ministry and is a public speaker, blogger, and hosts workshops for women and teen girls in which she seeks to provide an atmosphere in which they can Engage, Encourage, Enable, Edify and Exhale. Shanita can be contacted at realrawandrighteous@gmail.com

www.ingramcontent.com/pod-product-compliance
Lightning Source LLC
Chambersburg PA
CBHW060015050426
42448CB00012B/2763